This Book Belongs to

____

____

____

MERRY CHRISTMAS

Color Test

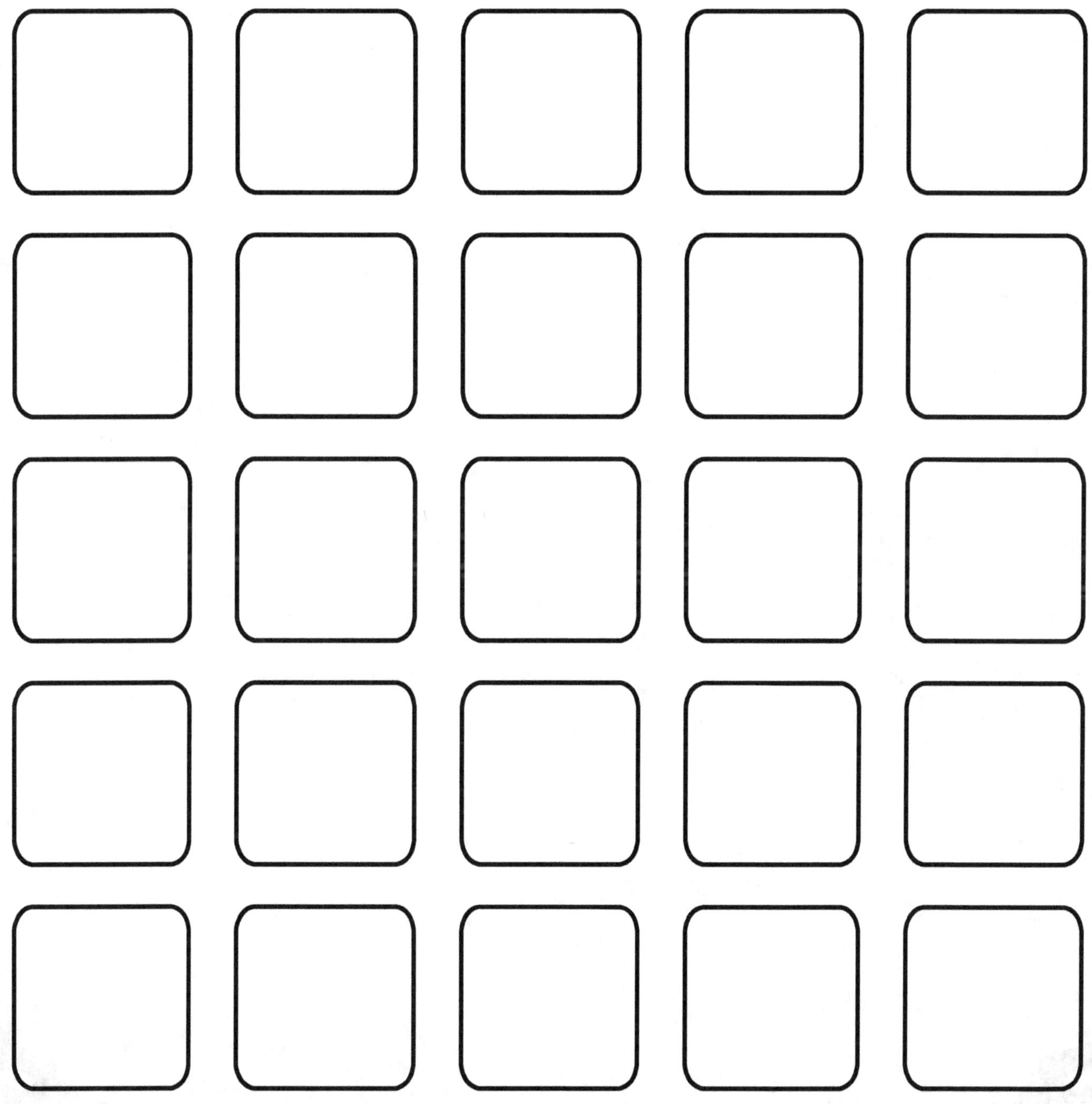

Merry Christmas

MERRY
CHRISTMAS

Merry
Christmas

Merry Christmas!

Merry Christmas!
Haappy New Year!

Merry Christmas!

Merry
CHRISTMAS!

MERRY CHRISTMAS

Merry Christmas!

Merry
Christmas

Merry Christmas

Merry Christmas

JOY
LOVE
PEACE
MERRY CHRISTMAS

INVITATION

Merry Christmas

Merry Christmas

Merry Christmas
Gifts
Let it Snow
Happy Holidays
Wishes

HAPPY HOLIDAYS